we touch the sky

BOOKS BY ROD McKUEN

POETRY

AND AUTUMN CAME
STANYAN STREET & OTHER SORROWS
LISTEN TO THE WARM
IN SOMEONE'S SHADOW
CAUGHT IN THE QUIET
FIELDS OF WONDER
AND TO EACH SEASON
COME TO ME IN SILENCE
MOMENT TO MOMENT
CELEBRATIONS OF THE HEART
BEYOND THE BOARDWALK
THE SEA AROUND ME . . .
COMING CLOSE TO THE EARTH
WE TOUCH THE SKY

COLLECTED POEMS

TWELVE YEARS OF CHRISTMAS
A MAN ALONE
WITH LOVE . . .
THE CAROLS OF CHRISTMAS
SEASONS IN THE SUN
ALONE
* THE ROD MCKUEN OMNIBUS
* THE WORKS OF ROD MCKUEN Vol. 1 (poetry) ●
HAND IN HAND
LOVE'S BEEN GOOD TO ME

PROSE

FINDING MY FATHER

COLLECTED LYRICS

NEW BALLADS●
PASTORALE●
THE SONGS OF ROD MCKUEN
GRAND TOUR●

* Published Only in the United Kingdom

W

ROD

Co
All
inc
in
Pu
A
Sin
Ro
12
N

T
g
b

S
F
P

Further information may be obtained by contacting the
Cheval/Stanyan Company, 8440 Santa Monica Boulevard, Los
Angeles, Ca. 90069, USA.

Jacket photograph by Edward Habib McKuen.

Typography and design by Hy Fujita.

Inside drawings and design by Hy Fujita and Rod McKuen.

Manufactured in the United States of America

1 2 3 4 5 6 7 8 9 10

Library of Congress Cataloging in Publication Data
McKuen, Rod.
  We touch the sky.

  "Cheval Books."
  I. Title.
PS3525.A264W4   811'.5'4   79–9419
ISBN   0-671-24828-6
ISBN   0-671-25183-X deluxe

Finally, for Jean
la vie, une vie

Only the birds
are able
to throw off
their shadows
—Vladimir Nabokov

CONTENTS

I have always thought of myself as a man of the elements, realizing that my best ideas and, for me, the nearest thing to knowledge have sprung from the realities of nature: the sea, the earth, the sky, rather than from books of history, religion or philosophy. And so, my life and work are filled with references to seashells, living close to the ground, ballooning, biplaning and hiking heavenward.

Fifteen years ago, I completed a trilogy of poetry and prose: The Sea, the Earth, and the Sky *to be read and recorded with music.* The Sea *contains many private thoughts that later formed the basis of a book,* Listen to the Warm. The Earth *was the genesis for such works as* Fields of Wonder *and* And to Each Season. *Few of the things I originally wrote for the album* The Sky *ever made their way into one of my books until now.*

The past five years of writing and rewriting, I've gathered together into a trilogy in book form some of the same elements I used in recording The Sea, The Earth, and The Sky. *Though meant as an overall work, each volume stems from a single encounter or idea. The books and records utilize the same canvas but are painted differently.*

In this final volume are eulogies for three friends who died in 1978. One killed himself before he reached the age of thirty, and appears near a poem I wrote about him in 1972. Another died just as he had passed his seventieth birthday. A third died at the age of forty-nine, outliving by ten years his doctor's expectations. For twenty years, in a partnership, we wrote words and music together. Now I continue to write verse for him.

R.M.
April 1979, New York City

CONTINUATION . . .

With one more hour
another day perhaps
a time of concentration
we could rise up
surpass, surprise ourselves
and all of our ambitions
maybe even thrust
an unclenched fist
through an empty cloud
or pass a golden galaxy
and with some patience
and no little practice
even touch the lower sky.

from "Coming Close to the Earth"

CLOUD BUSTING

BREAKING AND ENTERING

You've but to push your fist through mist and haze to penetrate the clouds. Easier for the dreamer, harder for airplanes.

The man who's dead to dreaming lives within a cloud of his own making and so his chance of entering the stratosphere is scant. I close my eyes to dreaming, only long enough to dream.

ELEMENTS

Each man rides the elements
or pauses in reviewing stands
as they pass by.

To know the sea
you must plunge into it
not once but often
till the water's foe or friend
          become a habit.

The quickest way
to learn the earth
is sifting ground
through ungloved hands.
Touching the sky
          is easy,
once you've found
          the ladder.

JUNE FLIGHT

Airborne—free
running with the sun
diving down the day
jumping through June—
Above the world
part of the shell
of some new world.

Now end over end
dipping with the down draft
hold on to me—I'm falling.
Catch me if I do.

Together
let us climb up
high enough to see
how much of heaven
            is reality
and what's invention.
Though no skybound ladder
            yet exists
your arms loose about me
seem a starting point.

They carry me aloft
when they encircle me.
I'm free while touching
just your forearm.

Those fragile, gentle arms
like vines that wind around
the strongest brick or board
till neither's sure
of who's supporting whom.

Stay awake.
We're flying now.
Don't let go
      nor will I.
The earth has moved
      beneath us
now it's gone.

COUNTRY POEM

Something pulls me
back and forth
across my country.

Seasons, yes
and seas at either end.
There are cities
I'm obliged to visit
in the business of business
                and curiosity
has more than once
been my travel guide,
but something deeper
tugs at me,
won't let me go.

It's as if my destiny
is to inch by inch myself
across the sprawling land
until my dust is ready
to mingle with the earth
I've run and crawled on
all my life.

Until then
I'll surely be a nomad
never finding roots
                or home
or always finding them
wherever journeys take me.

The push-pull
of the wind,
the magnet moon
that more than
once a month
fills up for me,
again the tides . . .
None would be enough.
Something more.

Nothing in a world
of pretty places
ever once approached
the love I have
for my own land.

I could not
catalogue or list
what I've found
          and find
within the borders
of my country.
It would take
another lifetime
to set down on paper.

With this first life
          half over
I cannot waste
the second half
in writing words
          of praise
or seeming propaganda.

But what a need
I sometimes feel
        to yell back
through the years
to Whitman—
Hey there, old man,
I hear your same America
and it is singing.

To visit Flat Rock
one more time
        and hunt up
Sandburg's ghost
just to reassure him
yes you made
our Lincoln live.
We go on loving
you as well as him.

I'd like to toss a pebble
in the pond at Walden Pond
and as it sank
and made an ever-growing
                        circle
Say Thoreau aloud
a thousand times
till all the birds
flew off to practice
calling out his name.

Again it's not
the great men only,
those who loved
the language and the land,
it's something else.

I suspect
that deep inside
my country's center
right or left of its
wide throbbing heart
the gravity's so strong
that none of us
will ever be
master or mistress
of our destiny,
especially knowing
that we're ill-equipped
to even half give back
what the sprawling land
        has given us.

LITTLE TOWNS AND PRETTY PLACES

Not the world's end
        or its beginning,
little towns and pretty places
are remembered lovingly
        and well.

Because we had the time
or took the time
to get to know them
they are the Calentes,
the Alamo Junctions
and the Somersets
of little worlds,
within our world.

Sometimes a certain tree
calls up the memory
of one whole town,
or the branch that broke
and survived two summers
as the whittled
             well-worn crotch
of a favored slingshot.

Jaw breakers
and red licorice candy,
the monthly present
when the grocery bill
was finally toted up
             and paid.

Somebody's skeleton
of somebody's kite,
dangling and flapping
month on month
from telephone-wire
         graveyards,
forgotten by the child
who lost it,
but a memory
and memorial to
those of us
who might otherwise
have relegated
to another head space
a town, a field,
that helped to form us.

The little towns
with one church spire
and half a congregation.

The pretty places
garlanded better
than they no doubt were
by our recollections
with inspired truth stretched
past the breaking point
of grown-up imaginations.

How much is true
I cannot know
            or speculate.
But while others
dwell on old Legionnaire picnics
or the day the sheriff's car
went through the window
            of the bon marché,

I remember clouds
arranged in special ways
or in a disarray of such design
it must have been deliberate
                and true.

In the little towns
I've traveled through
or settled in for summers
         or the week's end,
the pretty places
always seemed to be
above whatever hill
or high school campanile
dominated near and far
                horizons.

The pretty places
were the skies
whether filled with slender clouds
            or clustered ones
in bouquets or bunches.

Mostly after twilight
with no screened-off porch
or hammock swing
that might suggest a chance
                    for relaxation,
or in crowds
where others boast or brag
or put down hometowns
the memory starts.

Little towns
and pretty places
begin to dominate
the consciousness—when alone,
in conversation, or with company.

The loudmouth
or the school bully
remembers, embellishes,
talks often of the girls
he lured into the locker room
or settled down with in the tall grass.
The corporation head recalls
his peanut-butter-jelly lunch.

The inverted or the shy
remembers books that took
        four months to read.
And there are the endless stories
of certain grades—or high school plays,
Our Town, Our Hearts Were Young and Gay
The Nineteen-Fifty-Nine Review.

Harry, or was it Lionel
always won the lead
but couldn't make rehearsal
                after school
and still win on the football field.

I fall somewhere in between,
or not within a group at all.

Hung up on clouds
or wishing to be hanging there
I tell anyone who'll listen,
I suspect few do,
about the many mornings
that slid past mid-day
helped into long afternoons
by the most extraordinary clouds.

APRIL 1978/SOUTH OF MOSCOW

South of Moscow on the road to Susdal we passed great clusters of birch that alternated with pussy willow round and fuzzy even up above the April snow. I made them stop the car not once but twice so that I might gather armfuls of willow and bring them back to Pearl.

I knew that April would be difficult. So many anniversaries come that month and I was in another world, not just away from home. Breakfast every morning with Pearl and Bob made it easier. I never thought of you once. A dozen times a day, yes. Never once.

And John helped. And Elana, Maya, Mark and Roman and Fred and Sascha. They never knew it but they helped. You were past forgetting and they would insure that I would pass remembering off as just another accident in the young spring day.

APRIL IN THE EAST

Another field of snow
the sun begins to slice
each knoll or tree
that blocks its view
until it strikes a lake
and falls from sight.
I mourn its going
as I mourn the now gone day.

The birch so straight and strong
will not let the wildest storm
bend it to its knees,
one in every hundred hundred
is uprooted and falls down
and only then by accident.

The pussy willow
of this countryside
is new to me.
Not reeds this time
the way they have been
          all my life
but great trees
each bud an out-of-season
                    Christmas light.

Birds and beasts and man
are standing in a line
waiting for the thaw.
No sign as yet that April
will be anything
but parts and pieces
of December's past.

This winter
has been long.
Let the snow make up
new rivers not yet named
or reinforce the old ones,
let the green come sneaking
down the hills again
and climb the pines.
April be not March or Monday
            be yourself.

Yesterday
I tumbled
into Friday
missing half a week.
Even stones are hurrying
I don't know why.

AFTER STORM

Wave over wave
of simple sunlight
sets my eyes to dancing
or to staring straight ahead
hoping I can cause sun spots
to come together
in a single blue.
Not just a haze
      of happiness
           absolute
a steady blur so
it will make life even,
      if unreal.

OLD HOUSES

I love old houses
        for their smells,
their must and dust and mildew
and for what they've been
to people I will never know.

The character
of calked-up cracks
means more to me
than plastered walls and pretty paper,
walls that play the neighbors' music
when the radio I love
        has gone to sleep.

The faces of the old
are like old houses
every line's a highway
          from the past.

And so I love old houses
and the people who sit rocking
on their sagging porches.

OLD HOUSES, TWO

Back along the road to Moscow
                    and beyond
the dachas of one hundred years
            or more
have the character
of park bench people
feeding squirrels and pigeons
from paper bags and reticules.
Their lines have deepened
and will deepen more.

New coats of paint
will brighten them
and gloss on smiles
but the master painter still
is the brush and box
        of weather
and time the only artist
willing to take time.

It's proven on the fronts
of houses old and getting older
and the faces of the elderly
not old at all, but seasoned only.

Old faces
are the premier class.
Old houses closing in at second.
Not necessarily in age
but in history
undramatic but imposing.

Whistle me a tune
I ask a man
of undetermined
            years.
He does so
smiling afterward
as if no one
had thought to ask him
such a question
or put a like task
            to him
any time before.

I could drift along
the canal Grande
perceiving dwelling places
sinking slowly
and not feel sad.
Old houses earn
the right to die
to crumble
and be gone
with no tears shed.

OLD HOUSES, THREE

Somewhere in childhood
the pull of boarded buildings,
shacks and half-built mansions,
condominiums and constructions
                of every kind
began to seize me and even silence
disconnected tunes
that I was
humming
in my head.

Later while a drifter
I'd seek out
abandoned dwelling places,
moving in and dusting,
sometimes calking, walls
then papering them
with last week's newsprint.
I tried to make these
transient places home
for the duration of my stay
without disturbing
original intentions made by
the master or the mistress
who long ago decided on
yellow kitchens and flocked paper
                    in the hall.

Sometimes
even when a house
began to die beneath me
I stayed on. Even now
I can't abide the wrecker's ball
his booted army in destruction hats
his torch, his wrench, his crowbar.

COMING THROUGH THE TREES

For Camilla Snyder

COMING THROUGH THE TREES

Some years ago I finally saved enough to buy and build around me, a proper house. Through the years many places in that house, on those grounds, have become special to me—nothing more so than the window looking from my bathroom into pine trees. My security, every morning and part of every day when I'm at home. This year the trees were trimmed and thinned. Now wide paths of sunlight travel through the branches, not unlike a stained glass window. Even more birds come now and I feel more air.

THROUGH THE TREES

A saviour, maybe
        coming through the trees
a person not yet known to me.
Perception tells me it's a friend
                or will be.
How I know this
I am not exactly sure. But I do.

Within an open space I place a chair.
        Surely one who's come so far
        will find it useful
        as a resting place.
        Perhaps the sight
            of one lone chair
                will slow his walk.

We can talk if he is willing.
He is.
I see it in his gait.
Though coming forward
or standing still
he looms no larger
than at first.

Impatient, I arrange more chairs, four within a row. He may have friends who quietly bring up the rear.

For him a fifth and special chair
the color of the shadow he presents to me.

Horizons having slowed
and trees a mere mirage
the stranger too
has slipped into the mist
                or cloud.
I did not see him
                turning back,
so forward
he must finally come.

And now the chairs
I've placed across the road
are like a regiment.
A stumbling block,
a fence, a snare.

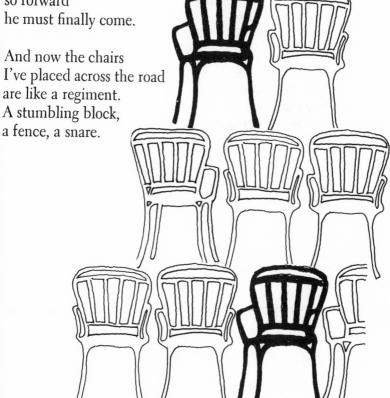

We move
from taking little interest
in our fellow man's ideals
his wants and needs
to the luxury
of never troubling
with any needs
but those
of our own selves.

What we need most
is some *one* else
while still remaining
resentful of intrusion.

Without the intercourse
            of conversation,
debate or non-debate,
whole sections of the brain
battle, blend and bleed
        are sealed off
and once the door is shut
on any hallway, in the head
it seldom opens up
                or out again.

I only wanted company.
Talk of weather
and the time of day.
No agenda planned
or Robert's Rules
need have been applied.

From year to year
it seems we graduate
from talking little
with each other
to talking not at all.

Come forward.
I am waiting still.
Perhaps this man
who briefly loomed
and then was lost
on the near horizon
has a Jean, a Helen
            or whatever
who tarried long enough
within his life
to love and be so loved
            then went away.

I have learned,
though late in life,
to listen and commiserate
            and I will.

POINT OF REFERENCE

Time is nothing without clocks.
Break the wristwatch
and the aging still continues.
but time grows muddled
                    and confused.
Pull the blind on sunshine
and the dark will keep us
in the middle night.
Without a calendar
we have only cold to show us
when the first full winter day
                    arrives.

The engine coughs, wheezes, stops,
the heart within the body
shrinks or slows
then finally halts,
the traffic light still works
or fails on unseen meters
based on timing and on time.
Time is nothing
without clocks.

SUN SPOTS

SUN SPOTS

It may be that an ordinary act of love makes us feel extra-ordinary—though what is so ordinary about an act of gentleness toward another, when we are told by preachers, teachers, and the over-reachers, of these times, that we should concern ourselves with self.

I allow no cult or culture as a stand-in, when I'm caught thinking just of me, I alone am guilty. The trick is being wise enough to catch myself. The treat is knowing some mistakes I've made, I'll not repeat again.

EXERCISE

Your bare shoulders,
young and lean
growing older
in the sun.

Turn slowly
so that I might see
your breasts again.

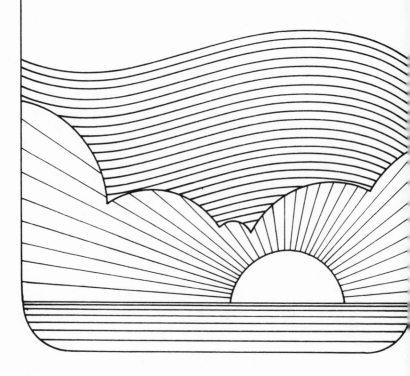

The corners of your eyes
but just the corners
                 frown.
You haven't smiled
and yet you do.

The sun's approval
won so easily
and he's been making
                 love to you
all day.
Aware of my turn now
he slips behind a cloud.

Later
I'll begin to make
new tunes for you,
music you can bend
       and sway to
while seducing tomorrow's
or the next day's sun.

Hurry now.
One virtue lacking
in my brain
       is patience.

SO LITTLE SUN

It may be that the sky
has no top at all
and love is only
        what it is—
the coming together
of people who need.

Finding out the names
of those among us
        we can trust.

Skies of every color
changing into other colors
          every day
but so little sun
to fill our black lives.

It may be that the sky
is layered differently
to every different eye
and some eyes
know a dozen different
colors of the sun.

My eyes
have lately
looked on you
      so often
they only see the sun
reflected in your own.

Stake me out a piece of blue,
light blue if you like
away from everything.

We'll go there and live,
above the rainbow stripes
between the layers
and the lids
of heaven.

THE BUTTERFLIES
ARE DRUNK ON SUNSHINE

The butterflies are drunk
              on sunshine
they weave and reel
against the garden wall
seeing no one,
imagining themselves unseen
they forage through
the budding fruit trees,
sigh and smile between
              snapdragons
and the phallic foxglove.

Behind the house
              and unaware
you paint your toenails
and frown at your reflection
in the dirty window glass
as I call out to you
coming from the porch.

So goes the summer
hour to hour, day to day.
You worry yourself
with something
that hasn't any name.

I pretend that worry
will not come into your eyes
unless I prop them open
with a kind of confidence
or will them to be so
with new indifference.

How can I presume such easiness
                                 with you
and still remain so insecure?

FLYING FREE

TWO WAYS OF FLYING FREE

ONE: HEADING UP

Up at 6 A.M., I track the near horizon while the sun is tracking me. Topping trees, and skimming lakes, hopping over barnyard fences like a skater on a pond trying to be dangerous by feigning figure 8's to gain attention. I never thought that I'd come any closer to the heavens than to climb a tree. But my balloon now lifts me higher than I've yet been lifted—takes me farther down the road than I've yet gone. I'm careful not to tamper with the unknown except to make it better known to me.

TWO: MOVING BEYOND

On Monday evening, the twenty-second of May, at exactly 9 P.M.—Pacific Daylight Time—Ralph James Wass went into a bean field across the street from his apartment in Costa Mesa, California, and placing a .38 caliber revolver against his head proceeded with a single shot to take his life. On the twentieth of July he would have been thirty years old. Though I will evermore be sad, I was not surprised to hear the news. It could not have been an easy journey to travel, lamb-like, in a world of wolves.

On the go, the twenty-ninth of April in New York City, I turned forty-five. That same morning in Moscow, Roman Karmen turned toward the wall and said: "I'm going," then, in agony, he died. He had passed seventy, but he should have gone to ninety-five. He worked toward his death, slowly, methodically and well. Ralph rode toward his in a Hudson or raced it on a motorcycle.

Then, Brel in autumn. It took ten years of death's round rattle before he finally stumbled and was gone. Despite official word, I know that he still walks the waterfront and sails the middle sea. Even now, he's perched upon the bedpost ready to advance another joke.

Though each man will now fly free, without them I feel bound.

114

BALLOON ONE: Perris, California

The first is up,
or going up.
It lifts off slowly.
Twin fires combine
like some eternal flame
to push and prod warm air
into that vast compartment
with its seven-story ceiling.

Soon the quiet,
soon the clouds,
as now another
tufted circle
     is entering
the angel's playground.

Two there are
they could be
harbingers of hundreds.
A space age army
          or armada
seeking space.

The grass still wet,
the sky just opening
woodchucks scatter in the lea
as foot by foot
and yard by cubic yard
the air is channeled
forced into another
and yet another
bright and billowing balloon.

Crows are crowing
hold the tether
don't let go
until we all let go.
Now douse the fire
and finish off the coffee.
The mist once heavy
as the heavens
        now subsides
as up we go—
fast at first
then slower, slow.

Below us
all the world
spreads out and opens.
Now, the sky
begins to glow
around, above us
        rim to rim
one horizon to another.

Dogs and children
chase our shadow.

Along the coastline
we dip to skim the water,
then rise higher to avoid
        an early splashdown.

Reach out and grab a handful
of the nearest cloud
as we sail even with
        now past the sun.

Far below
birds track our course.
If this is not land's end
        coming up,
I know no better
finish line.

BALLOON TWO: Durban, S.A.

Six A.M.
the chase truck's
        out of fuel.
Never mind
we'll still be in the sky
        by sunrise.
Seven and we're up.
Low hills first
and then green trees
a farmer shouts *come down*
and have a cup of tea
as on we sail.

Now a village
and the natives scatter.
We wave and bravely
they shout back,
hang on
while we slip
                slowly down
to top the trees.
Bumping, scraping
                    feather-like
the topmost branches.
You let loose
a Texas rebel yell.

Eight.
The morning sky
is now red diamonds
and as many different shapes
                    and sizes
as the sectioned fields.
We'll skim the lake
at left and just ahead,
or set down in the meadow
just below that far brown knoll.

            Not now.
A little higher first,
a little farther yet
surely something lies beyond, beyond,
                    beyond.

Look!

The chase truck's catching up.
Fire up again.
Beyond that grove
of blossoming trees
we'll *lose* it.

     Stand still, look up
           then scatter
over half a dozen acres.

      Three white birds below us
pay no attention
as our shadow scrapes them
    like a passing cloud.

Not quite nine.
Two fuel tanks still unused
we can sail straight through
The Valley of a Thousand Hills
and not come down till noon.

The trees we're topping now
              have only tops.
Above
the slightly superstitious sun
plays hide-and-seek
but warms us anyway.
The day is opening
now hills beyond
              the front hills
show themselves
              as we come near.

Cane fields
stretch out
    along the left
on the right side
      chicken farms
        and chicken farms.

Unexpectedly,
more clouds ahead.

A black girl running
            down the road
hides behind
        the sugar stalks
peering at this aberration
                    in the sky
confident that she
    can spy on us
        and not be seen.

We let her keep her secret
and wonder what she'll tell
her unbelieving friends.

Hau! Did you see?
Men looking,
but they couldn't find me.
They fly in painted egg
they cook it
light the fire.

Hau! A big egg.
In many colors.

Hau! In the sky!
I threw it with a stone.
Hau! Egg run away.

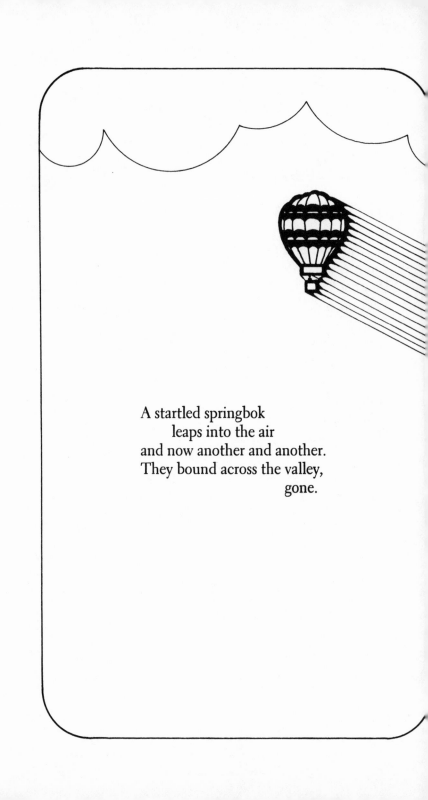

A startled springbok
    leaps into the air
and now another and another.
They bound across the valley,
            gone.

RALPH
(Written in spring 1972)

Someone wrote of you
that people work a lifetime
to attain your natural innocence.
I believe that to be so,
for on seeing you
the first time out
I remember that I felt
as though I'd come upon
the living Christ.

I'm sure that when
His tongue was tangled
Christ nodded out of shyness
and that He needed other men
as you do.

You have to be a man
to care for other men.
Isn't that why God built flesh
around the spirit of His son
and made Him visible?

Jesus on a motorcycle,
hair helmetless and blowing
in the hard wind,
eyes flattened back
against His face,
riding through the northern night
safe inside the skin of Ralph.

RALPH JAMES WASS (1948–1978)

I loved you Ralph
not as disciples
love their Christ
but as one man
grows to love another
            for himself
and for what he
cannot be himself.

I never knew you
to be mean
            or petty.
Can I say that
            of anyone
that I know now?

You must have needed
                someone
in that final hour,
I wasn't there—
and I was one
of only five
who gathered
to remember you
an hour before
the wind received
                your ashes
between the coast of Catalina
and the mainland.

Christ had his disciples
and there was one
                among us
who killed you too.
He halted just this side
of pulling back the trigger.

While rummaging
amid the little that you left us
(there were no photographs
and all the negatives
          were fuzzy),
I found a silver ring
that you had hollowed out
and made with your own hands,
it hasn't left my finger since
and you, yourself, continue
pounding in my heart.

The loss of you
is compounded
by my inattention
in the months
before you took your life,
you're now held up
as idol and a blueprint
for how I think
all of us
who come into the world
          from wherever
should treat each other.

WHY I'M WALKING
THROUGH THE UNKNOWN WAR

Long dead old women
clinging to their lives
in nineteen forties Leningrad,
young mothers, after factory shifts,
making cookies out of rancid flour
                    and turpentine.

Children licking paste
from off the papered walls,
to live another springtime
to laugh another fall.
And all the while the winter,
like a hundred thousand miles
of unscarred birch moves in.

Trucks skate across
the frozen Ladoga
with their ammunition cargo,
held down by curled
                    and flapping canvas.

Children now criss-cross the ice
                        pulling coffins
off to bury yesterday's dead family,
their own they hardly got to know.
Thrown up on the screen,
this newsreel footage
                        ten feet wide
three times that age
is newer than the newspaper
lying lifeless next to me.
Finally I close my eyes
more in desperation
                        than in rest.
Young men's faces in a line
captured by the frozen lens
                        of Roman Karmen—
all dead now
even if they once survived
three winters at the front.

I think of birch trees
with new bark,
the music of it
already starting in my ears.
Spring buds everywhere
children full and smiling
but still that line of faces
will not leave my head.

Twenty-one flights up
the snow in New York's newest
                    blizzard
swirls amid the concrete canyons
and falls to where I'll find it
within the coming hour
piled in four-foot drifts
as I hike the two long blocks
to my warm hotel.
Again that line
of young men's faces
not one resigned
                    or undetermined.

It seems to me
the living owe the dead—
those struck down
by known or unknown wars
a viewing or an overview.
Even though we cannot see,
the holocaust through
                their dead eyes,
there should be
a telling of it
even if it's but a try.

ROMAN KARMEN (1906–1978)

Roman,
let this be your epitaph,
I tried and I succeeded
down a lifetime,
      round a world
from peace to peace
only by coincidence
        war to war.

But epitaphs
are not enough
when the moss
has finally covered
you and your high-walled
        resting place
that soft green comforter
will be as safe for you
as any honor guard
or well-locked gate.

Last year
as I was finishing
the work that you
            allotted me
I always felt
your breath upon my neck
heavy if you seemed
to disagree with my way
            of doing things
light—and almost never there
when I knew you gave
            approval.

And how your friends
          resisted me,
protecting you
and all their memories
even at your death.

It is the measure
of a man well loved
when friends left behind
become caretakers
of such elusive things
          as dreams
not fully realized.

Sleep well.
For your ideas
        and ideals
belong to all your countrymen
and they will protect
the lessons and the need
                    to know
even if the teacher's
        moved ahead.
The seeds of Socrates
have never stopped
            repopulating.

So it will be
and so it is
with what you've left.

What you may not know
or never realized
is that you narrowed
                boundaries
and some have even
come down altogether
in the year
that you've been gone.

From "I'M NOT AFRAID"
(Jacques Brel – Rod McKuen – 1969)

What is for real?
What is false?
All of us seem to be
caught in a waltz
turning around,
          turning again.
When will the dancing
               ever end
as for us, you and me
our eyes are open
we can see
both of us know
where we've been
why must we both
go dancing again
are you afraid,
I'm not afraid . . .

JACQUES BREL (1929–1978)

Reason is
the shortest road
        to freedom.
Poets know that
even in the midst
        of dreaming
or trying out
our songs upon ourselves.

And poets always go
in quest of freedom
not just for themselves
but for every man
whose mind has been
        too long in chains.

I learned
the worth of freedom
from your mutterings
                and frowns
even now I see you
looking up from some
                newspaper
to read aloud today's injustice
pausing on the peeks
                of paragraphs
to wonder how the world
or one man anywhere
can offer cruelty
for lack of courage.

Love is
the only easy way
              through life.
And who'd have thought
that such an easy road
is paved, repaved
and used so often.

The *chansonier*
will tell you
which road is the sure one
and he's dependable
as guide and go-for,
because he wants
              to get there too.

I learned
the worth of love
from all the many ways
            you said it.
Pound for pound
more ways of loving
came from you
than all the hate
most men amass
throughout their lifetimes.

You left behind
so many primers
on the subject
that generations
coming up
then moving to oblivion
will find life's starting place
            with greater ease.

But dammit—
there are far too many
mysteries you made off with,
mornings you took with you,
that none but you will know.

I envy all those unlearned couplets
you hadn't yet set down.
Instructions to the world
and even some to me.

Now only JoJo
will hear you laugh
and share again your private language.

If only I'd have been there
                for that final minute,
just to say *Ne me quitte pas*.

IN SUMMING UP

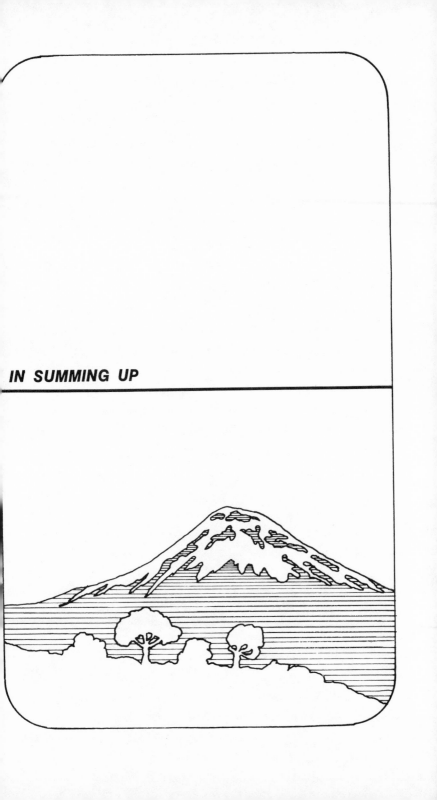

RUNNER

I have no time to hate, I'm in a hurry.
But I've got all the hours in the days
still left to me to waste on love.
And what a waste of God's free time to
not love readily and straight ahead.

IN SUMMING UP

It's a long way back
        to San Francisco
and the starting point
where I learned
to make up truths
and make them so
for those who shared
my pillow and my life.

I know that I'm accountable
and that the bill
is adding up
mounting like a hill
of shifting grain.

One day I'll come
          face to face
with bigger animals than I
then I'll be carried off
the way the cats
were taken by coyotes
from the backyard hill
          one summer.

Till then
even if it's only my own words
that keep me company
          I'm not alone.

The animals are coming
          and I wait.

PHASE THREE

I think I'm managing
the turn quite well
I'm almost sure of it
I even find myself
greedy for the coming day.

I'm stronger now
because of time and
                thunder.
Without the push
       of thunder
and the grace of time
I would still be looking,
but always with a sense of hope
               and wonder.

I can handle hope
as well as heartache
life as well as living—
(how unalike they are
as different in their way
as death and dying) .

I can keep a smile on
long past its due
and think beyond
the time of thinking
once the process has been
                    set in motion.

The elements
did that for me.
The sea, the earth, the sky
(created by God in that order)
are not unlike a well-served meal
                   and in that order.

At first the fish or soup,
followed by red meat
that only lately stalked the ground.
To finish off the dinner
in a proper way, fowl,
the partridge or the quail
knocked lifeless from the sky.

A lesson in all things.
Morning, afternoon and night,
youth, the middle years and age.
Even the blessed trinity
was manufactured in a *three*.

God worked in order,
leaving us to sort out
some order for ourselves.

I have the *sea* around me,
however wild it's there
                and it's dependable.
When I come closer to the *earth*
I'm able out of true reality
to assess my proper worth,
without extremities or exaggerations.

Though it takes
the hardest effort
to reach the heavens,
when finally
we touch the *sky*
contentment like a cloud
will suddenly surround us.
                Trust me.

About the Author

Rod McKuen's books of poetry have sold in excess of 17,000,000 copies in hardcover, making him the best-selling and most widely read poet of our times. In addition, his poetry is taught and studied in schools, colleges, universities, and seminaries throughout the world.

Mr. McKuen is the composer of over 2,000 songs which have been widely translated. They include: "Jean," "Love's Been Good to Me," "The Importance of the Rose," "Rock Gently," "Ally, Ally, Oxen Free," and several dozen songs written with the late French composer Jacques Brel, including "If You Go Away," "Come Jeff," "Port of Amsterdam," and "Seasons in the Sun." Both writers have termed their writing habits together as three distinct methods: collaboration, adaptation, and translation.

Mr. McKuen's film music has twice been nominated for motion picture Academy Awards ("The Prime of Miss Jean Brodie" and "A Boy Named Charlie Brown"), and his classical works are performed by the world's leading orchestras. In May, 1972, the London Royal Philharmonic premiered his Concerto No. 3 for Piano and Orchestra and a suite, "The Plains Of My Country." In 1973 the Louisville Orchestra commissioned Mr. McKuen to compose a suite for orchestra and narrator entitled "The City." It was subsequently nominated for a Pulitzer Prize.

His Symphony No. 3, commissioned by the Menninger Foundation in honor of their fiftieth anniversary, was premiered in 1975 in Topeka, Kansas. Recently he completed the libretto and music for The Black Eagle. He calls the full-length work a "Gothic" musical.

In July 1976 two new McKuen works were premiered at St. Giles Church, Cripplegate, in the City of London. A Concerto for Cello and Orchestra and the first major symphonic composition written for synthesizer and symphony orchestra: Concerto for Balloon and Orchestra. In April of 1979, the composer-author had three full-length ballets premiered in Pittsburgh. He is presently composing music and the libretto for three more ballets to be produced in Pittsburgh during the coming season.

Last year Mr. McKuen was named by the University of Detroit for his humanitarian work and in Washington was presented The Carl Sandburg Award by the National Platform Association as "the outstanding people's poet, because he has made poetry a part of so many people's lives in this country."

For nearly a year Mr. McKuen has taken a sabbatical from concerts and touring to work on the television documentary series The Unknown War as poet, composer of the film's score, and co-adapter, with producer Fred Weiner, of the scripts.

Having recently taken up residence in New York, the composer-poet now divides his time between Manhattan and the California coast.